W9-BPK-728

ISBN 88-7057-099-1

Printed in Italy by Grafiche Lema - Maniago Pn

ITALY
a journey of dreams

Photography by
H. SIMEONE HUBER

Text by
MATTEO COLLURA

Translated by
JOHN G. HARPER

MAGNUS

seat of a car: Florence, Venice, Rome, Siena, Bologna, Pisa, Mantua, Palermo and Naples – each of these towns is well worth a visit, even if one has to travel half-way round the world to do so. The sheer concentration of works of art in Italy is miraculous, no other nation on our planet has anything to match it. This in turn leads to another much discussed problem: respect for this heritage and the best ways of presenting and "using" it. This is very delicate and controversial ground, fraught with such problems as shameful neglect, blind and sometimes criminal speculation, and misunderstood progress. Too many works of art, too many noble monuments have been ruined, mutilated and devoured, sacrificed to the haphazard advance of modern building schemes. But having said this, it must be admitted that many architectural treasures have been saved and many will be saved. Venice and Florence still remain almost intact to enchant us with their urban architecture, to amaze us with their cornucopian museums, and to fascinate us with their unique scenography.

Art and Nature: the two go so well together in Italy. The Florentine basilica of Santa Maria del Fiore rises up in an urban context fashioned by the hands of famous architects, but it is also framed by an exquisite countryside which is universally considered to be a work of art in itself; the ruins of the residence of the Roman Emperor Tiberius on Capri dominate one of the most extraordinary panoramas that sea, sky and land can possibly offer, and the same is true of the ruins of the Greek Theatre at Taormina. There is no corner of Italy which is not worth seeing, apart from, of course, those recent urban agglomerations which are springing up all over the world and not just afflicting Italy.

One thing that usually astonishes a first time visitor to Italy is the majesty of her mountains, for many people imagine that it is a country of monuments and golden beaches. It is not only the Alps which are so impressive, but also the "surprising" Appennines and the vast mountain ranges of Sicily which take up so much of the island and about which so little is known. It is not by pure chance or the whim of some southern Italian that the *biscotti dello sciatore* (skiers' biscuits) is not a speciality of the Alto Adige or the Val d'Aosta but of a village which nestles at the foot of Mount Etna. So there are many "Italies", as many as there are towns, and no doubt someone will say as many as there are Italians, but one cannot deny the cultural independence of every province and every city. To realise this it is only necessary to visit some of the village and town fetes, each with their own jousts and contests, which enliven life in Italy. Every *quartiere,* every borough, has its own patron saint, its own Madonna, just as every square inch of land is connected to some part of history, be it small or great. So Italy is beautiful, but it is also contradictory, paradoxical, complicated. Things become even more complicated when one realises that perhaps beside some venerable ruin, there are some parts of Italy more American than even America itself, and is there anwhere more modern than that?

Matteo Collura

Take a map of Europe and a pair of compasses and put the point on, let's say, Milan. Open out the compasses until the other leg touches Ragusa, in Sicily. Keeping the point on Milan bring the arc of the radius towards the north, passing through the North Sea, and you will arrive at a point on the border between Germany and Denmark. This little experiment is to demonstrate just how "long" Italy actually is: the distance from Milan to Ragusa is the same as that from Milan to Flensburg, a city in the northern part of the Federal Republic of Germany. This latitudinal "extension" helps to explain the enormous variety of landscape and climate, but there are other facts which must be understood when one talks of Italy, such as the effect of its geographically central location in Europe, or its politically strategic position, which has attracted or drawn so many different races to its territory, which, as a consequence, has had to absorb or assimilate many different civilizations.

Forming a natural bridge between Europe and Africa and between East and West, Italy is a land of alliances and misalliances, conflicts and treaties, where the Byzantine mosaics flourish between Gothic arcades, and the rough impact of the northern tribes was softened by the calming influence of Alexandrian refinement, for there are more traces of the ancient Greek civilization to be found in Italy than in Greece itself. Italy is a nation where the history of the land is told by the very walls of the cities, where the countless ruins which stud the landscape from the mountains in the north to the very tip of Sicily tell of splendid adventures and devastating tragedies; it is a land so saturated by the past that its inhabitants have become part of the historical process, individuals who are so accustomed to living beside magnificent monuments and priceless works of art that they are hardly aware of them any more. It is not by chance or sheer coincidence that much of Italy's architectural heritage, its discovery and preservation is thanks to the efforts of those travellers from north of the Alps who in the 18th and 19th centuries set out on their cultural or romantic journeys to the land of the silver-green olive trees and terraced vineyards. Whatever their reasons for undertaking this often hazardous adventure were, they were often rewarded with the apparition of elegant capitals, broken statuary and ornate cornices among the goats and gorse-bushes. No other nation in the Old World has been so dreamed of, so desired, so yearned for. How many intellectuals from other lands have come here on pilgrimages? How many accounts have they written of their "wonder", of their amazement. The historical strata of Italy are so deep that when he was in Assisi, Wolfgang Goethe felt entirely justified in "skipping" the Giotto frescoes of the Basilica of St. Francis in order to be able to dedicate more time to the Augustan temple of Minerva which was so much more pertinent to his study of classicism. About thirty years later Stendhal thought it was sufficient to write just a few lines about the treasures of Florence and did admit that Rome had a "sweet climate" but was full of praise for the beautiful Neoclassical architecture of Milan. So there is an Italy for all tastes. But it is also a demanding country, especially if one is an artist. When one reads the biographies of famous painters and sculptors one can be sure of coming across, sooner or later, passages which go a bit like this: "I always thought I could do this well until I visited Rome and saw my first Michelangelo," or "...until I went to Florence and came across my first Masaccio...".

Even though Italy has had a veritable host of admirers who have raved about the delights of Capri, Asolo, and Cortina, as well as the more obvious cities such as Venice, Florence and Rome, there are many wonderful places which were not discovered – perhaps "contaminated" might be a better word – until very recently. This is true for Basilicata or certain parts of Abruzzo and Calabria, not to mention Sardinia – until a few years ago a neglected and forgotten island and still mysterious even today – and many other parts of Italy which are known only to those who actually live there.

Travelling in this "minor Italy", which may not be able to boast of glorious monuments or splendid altar-pieces but which is never more than a brief detour away from the more obvious tourist haunts, one meets a people who cannot merely be summed up by the two adjectives which are usually employed to describe Italians – "hospitable and creative". Of course most Italians are just this, but after travelling across the depopulated lands of the South, or *mezzogiorno,* or after visiting the devastated and over-exploited country-side of the Veneto and Friuli, it is necessary to admit that they are also extremely hard-working and courageous – qualities that have taken or driven them to every corner of the world. This is one of the paradoxes of the nation: on the one hand it expresses, in a most refined and elegant way, the art of knowing how to enjoy life, an art which has always fascinated foreigners and for which they envy us, on the other hand we have had the "diaspora", or dispersion, painful and fraught, the emigration of the population which at the turn of the century reached biblical proportions.

One often hears this word "paradox" when travelling around Italy. I explained this before: the very length of the territory brings about sharp surprising contrasts in landscape and climate, whilst the "piling-up" of different civilizations, one on top of the other, has resulted in a population which could never be called homogeneous. It is useful to consider one very important fact if one really wishes to understand Italy, and to explain this I have borrowed the words of Giuseppe Antonio Borgese: "The Italian nation has its origins, like all the other nations of Europe, in the Late Middle Ages, but it was born in a totally different way. Italy was not created by kings or generals, it was the creation of a poet: Dante." A nation which owes its life, as it were, to a poem, whose unity was constructed from a poetic creation, cannot but have its own special characteristics and peculiarities in which art plays an essential role. This is why Italian tourism, even when it reaches massive proportions as it does on the Adriatic coast, is always enlightened by culture. Italians are quick to boast that the towns they live in are "cities of art", but more often than not they are speaking the truth. Cities of art, open museums and art galleries which can even be enjoyed from the

Venice, Piazzetta di San Marco with the island of San Giorgio in the background. A city which is loved by artists and lovers – one could even say built for them – Venice is an urban agglomerate which is unique in the world. Nowhere except here, in this gallery of unforgettable vistas, exists such an equilibrium between water and land, canals and footpaths. Venice consists of hundreds of islands and is criss-crossed by 177 canals, which reach 45 kilometres in length. The most important canal is the most beautiful because it is packed with precious churches and sumptuous palaces, it is rightly called the Grand Canal.

By sheer miracle Venice has remained almost untouched and intact for centuries. One can see today the same views which were admired in Renaissance times. This is due to its particular urban configuration, but also to the impossibility of using any type of motorised transport, except of course for boats, gondolas, motor-lauches and passenger boats. A theatre-city, totally Italian, Venice is for many months of the year crowded with tourists. In the summer Piazza and Piazzetta San Marco throng with an excited multicoloured mass, but these dense surging crowds seem miles away from the peace which reigns in the hidden squares and alleys, which provide a refuge for those who know the city better than the transient tourist.

Venice, the gondolas tied up in front of Piazzetta San Marco with the dome of Santa Maria della Salute in the background. The magical light of the morning burnishes this cameo of Venice, beloved by painters. The brilliant and most original idea of the 17th century Venetian architect Baldassare Longhena the Salute was built to commemorate the victory over the terrible plague, but it is also an exultation of the cult of the Virgin Mary.

Venice – *acqua alta,* or high-tide, in Piazzetta San Marco. An amphibious city, Venice has inevitably developed a love-hate relationship with the water. Ever since it was founded the city has had to struggle with the estuaries of the rivers, which, if not checked, would have inevitably silted up the lagoon. For this reason the Venetians changed the course of the rivers, moving the estuaries far away from the city. This struggle continues still, and in fact is a major problem in this time of hydro-geological upheavals. Venice is now undergoing an extremely critical period, and not surprisingly, the whole world has united its energies to save it, because the Serenissima is not only the pride of Italy, but of the whole world.

Venice, Ca' d'Oro. An important example of Venetian Gothic architecture from the 15th century, this imposing palace, whose decorations seem like battlements, stands on the Grand Canal and today houses an important museum. Here can be seen Mantegna's *San Sebastiano,* Van Dyk's *Portrait of a Gentleman,* and Guardi's *Piazzetta di San Marco;* as well as paintings by Carpaccio, Giovanni Bellini and Filippo Lippi.

Passariano (Udine): Villa Manin, architectural jewel of the eighteenth century. This immense palace was built as a monument to the grandeur of the family and as a magnificent foretaste of the wonders of Venice. Villa Manin was in fact a customary stop for travellers coming from beyond the Alps on their way to the capital of the Serenissima. The

building, provided with a wide circular court, also served for the gathering and storage of agricultural products before they were sent to markets all over the world. The first plans for the villa seem to have been drawn up by Baldassare Longhena, but in the 18th century the building, through the intervention of Giovanni Ziborghi, took on its present sumptuous aspect which makes one think of such places as Vienna or Versailles. In the salons on the ground floor there are frescoes by Ludovico Dorigny, and plaster-work and paintings carried out in the Austrian Rococo style.

Villa Manin: one of the many famous villas of the Veneto, which constitute one of the most beautiful itineraries of art that North Italy can offer. It begins with the buildings designed by Palladio in the 16th century, and ends with, as in the example of Villa Manin, with those built two centuries later. It is a truly amazing series of architectural splendours, a "phenomenon" as James S. Ackerman, Professor of Art at the University of Harvard, explains: "During the formative years of the villa and *villeggiatura,* Venice became increasingly aware of her role as heir to ancient Rome. The Venetian villas drew their inspiration from Roman models, even though the builders Renaissance Venice could have had no first-hand experience of the architecture of ancient Rome. The villas of Palladio illustrate the complexity of this civilization which combined the results of research on the surviving Roman monuments with the traditional elements of Venetian agricultural architecture and forms which derived from mediaeval castles."

Cortina d'Ampezzo, with the Cristallo's Group in the background. We are here in the so-called "Pearl of the Dolomites", the mountainous chain which takes its name from the man who discovered its particular mineralogical composition, the Frenchman Dolomieu. With its unsurpassed location – and so preferred by constructors of hotels and houses which are not always built in a style suitable to the environment – not only is Cortina the ski-ing venue for enthusiasts from all over the world, but also for all sorts of tourists who can find, in this part of the upper valley of the Boite, a first-class social life and every type of sporting activity. Cortina offers an immensely varied choice of ski-runs and landscapes. In the summer it provides an excellent stopping place for those who are touring the Strada delle Dolomiti, the beautiful road from Bolzano to Misurina, passing through Canazei and the mountain passes of Pordoi and Falzarego.

Trentino Alto Adige: the Cimone della Pala (3,185 m.) inflamed by the setting sun, as seen from Passo Rolle. The Cimone, due to its shape, is also called the *Cervino delle Dolomiti* (the Matterhorn of the Dolomites).

A flower-covered meadow in the **Dolomites.** Spring and summer in these mountains, which are considered by many to be the most beautiful in the world, are witness to an explosion of vivid colours which herald the end of the long season of ice and snow. The flora of the Dolomites are renowned for their variety and beauty, and even on the rock-strewn plateaus high above the lush meadows intrepid climbers are often rewarded with glimpses of exquisite flowers.

Trentino Alto Adige, Val di Funes, the village of Santa Maddalena with the Odle peaks in the background. The Val di Funes (Villnöstal), which runs parallel to the Val Gardena, is inhabited mainly by German-speaking people. This is a very special part of Italy, due principally to the fact that it is one of the few places where the inhabitants actually have their origins in that area instead of having settled there from some distant land, which is the case for most other parts of the country. These Alpine landscapes are very different from the traditional and popular image of Italy as a land of sun, sea, and picturesque monuments, but this is such a varied and unpredictable land that scenes very similar to this can be found in the Sila Calabra, in the southernmost part of Italy, and in certain parts of the Sicilian

Nebrodi, far way in Sicily. Italy, more than any other nation, can offer a surprising variety of regions. For traditional and practical reasons it has been divided into the north, the centre, and the south, but many of the regions in the north are quite different from their neighbours, and the same is true for the centre and for the south.

Merano, Castle Tirolo, with the Val d'Adige in the background. Merano was the capital of the Tyrol before Innsbrück, and only became part of Italy after the First World War, in fact it still preserves much of its Austrian atmosphere. It was a well-known tourist resort back in the 19th century thanks to its hot springs, which are once again proving popular with visitors. Merano is also famous for the Gran Premio horse races which are held every September against a spectacular backdrop of valleys and mountains.

Lago di Garda (also known as Lago di Benaco) is the largest of all the Italian lakes – so large in fact that from some places it seems more like a sea. It covers an area of 370 square kilometres, is 51 kilometres long and 17.5 kilometres wide. Lake Garda is probably the ideal synthesis of all that is wonderful on our peninsula. The mildness of the climate in the area around the lake is legendary, permitting the cultivation of olives, whose delicate silver-green leaves are in contrast to the glossy dark green foliage of the orange and lemon trees, which also grow well here.
Dotted along the shores of the lake are towns

whose names have become famous, such as Sirmione, Desenzano, Salò, Gardone, Peschiera, Lazise, and Riva. The Roman poet Catullus was captivated by the beauty and mildness of Garda, and was especially enchanted by Sirmione ("Paeninsularum, Sirmio, insularumque Ocelle...").

Verona, Ponte Pietra: in the background stands the church of Santa Anastasia. Verona is the city where Shakespeare set his famous tragedy *Romeo and Juliet,* and this is one of the reasons why it has become a traditional rendez-vous for lovers and newly-weds. If you want to see the famous balcony just go to Via Capello 23, right in the heart of the old city. A town rich in history, Verona was the most important centre of Northern Italy under the Romans. Notable architectural monuments dating from that time are the Porta dei Borsari, the Theatre, and of course the Arena, which in the summer acts as host to a highly esteemed and amazingly spectacular opera season. The plan of the city, notwithstanding the passing of the centuries, remains very much the same as it was in Roman times, with its centre at Piazza delle Erbe, which used to be the old Roman forum. Verona can also boast of an impressive amount of Romanesque architecture such as the church of San Fermo Maggiore, and the church of San Zeno, which has been rebuilt seven times, the last time being in the 12th century.
A very prosperous city, Verona has managed to preserve many of the characteristics it acquired when it formed part of the Serenissima. Guido Piovene in his *Viaggio in Italia* shrewdly observes: "They say Verona is romantic and picturesque, and therefore a bit provincial; it is in fact a great city, a capital city, and a provincial city at the same time. It is a city which is still the capital of an enormous kingdom called a province, which, as often happens in Italy, possesses the vitality and energy of a metropolis. In no other city in the Veneto is there such a feeling of liveliness, vivaciousness, and the sensation that the people are actually enjoying life; in this respect it can perhaps be compared to Naples, but fortunately it does not possess the dark, squalid poverty-stricken side of that city. Poetry written in the old Venetian dialect is very popular here, and the Venetian *maschera* (mask), which can be both peasant and aristocratic, learned and improvised, knowing and flighty, and which has disappeared from the rest of the region, still has a strong foothold here."

Padua, Prato della Valle, with the Basilica of Santa Giustina in the background. There is an old saying which goes: *Veneziani gran signori, padovani gran dottori...* which means that the Venetians, thanks to their maritime commerce, have amassed great wealth and become *gran signori,* or great lords; the Paduans, on the other hand, thanks to their ancient University, have amassed great wealth and a level of learned culture which is equally impressive. It is true that Padua owes much of its fame to its University, founded long ago in 1222: Petrarch and Dante were just two of the many students who studied here and who were later to become famous.

Prato della Valle, one of the centres of the city, consists of a large oval garden surrounded by a moat and overlooked, or perhaps guarded, by 78 statues of some of the University's famous alumni. Even today this enormous square, reputed to be one of the largest in Europe, is one of the important social gathering points for the *Padovani,* even though the thundering preachers and rowdy but colourful jousts of bygone days have given way to the endless ebb and flow of today's traffic and the inevitable market stalls. The vastness of Prato della Valle forms a perfect setting for the severe but imposing mass of the Basilica of Santa Giustina, which dates from the 4th century but whose facade was rebuilt in the 16th century. Padua is also famous for the capella degli Scrovegni, where some of Giotto's most famous and impressive frescoes can be admired.

Ravenna, a detail of the mosaics of the Basilica of San Vitale, showing Queen Theodora and her court. Ravenna, a city of Emilia-Romagna near the Adriatic Sea, possesses a concentration of mosaic decorations which has no equal in the world, not even in the Orient.

As soon as you arrive in the city you will be told to visit the tomb of Dante, a monument which in fact does very little justice to the poet; instead you should pass your time admiring the splendours of the Byzantine mosaics, a shimmering explosion of golds, blues, greens and reds which no other pictorial technique can reproduce. It is as if in the Basilica of San Vitale or the Mausoleum of Galla Placidia, or in Sant'Apollinare Nuovo or Sant'Apollinare in Classe, every single piece of mosaic is contributing to create an immense symphony; they saturate the apses, naves, transepts, vaults and arcades with their magical orchestration of glittering colours.

Mantua. The structure of this elegant Lombardian city is considered to be a miracle of hydrological science. The first dwellings were erected on some of the islands which rise up out of the waters of the river Mincio, which, winding its way through marshlands, widens out to form a lake. With the passing of centuries this lake was divided into three parts and the waters were channeled according to the changing and expanding urbanistic needs of the area.

Birthplace of Virgil, Mantua is a city which, behind its fortified walls which are scarred by a proud and troubled past, can boast of numerous artistic treasures. Amongst the most well-known of these is the Palazzo Ducale, a complex of buildings composed of five-hundred rooms and fifteen courtyards. A large part of the decorations was carried out under the orders of the Gonzaga family who, during their long reign, summoned to Mantua the best artists of Italy. The *Camera degli Sposi* (the Room of the Bridle Couple), with frescoes by Andrea Mantegna, draws crowds of visitors.

Milan, the Duomo (Cathedral). This immense creation in marble is the symbol or emblem of the Lombardian industrial, commercial and financial hub of Italy. An imposing Gothic temple whose construction began in 1386, it is 140 metres long and, at the transepts 85 metres wide. Successive generations of architects and stonemasons were employed during its construction; the facade was finally completed in 1858. The famous Madonna was placed on top of the church in the second half of the 19th century. Dimly lit by the mediaeval stained-glass windows, the interior is a triumph of emotional majesty. The pillars of the nave and its four aisles make up a veritable forest of soaring pillars. The remains of San Carlo Borromeo are conserved in the crypt.

A city which has become a synonym for its hectic social life and economic opulence, Milan is still the "moral" capital of Italy, not to be confused with Rome, which is only the "political" capital. The writer Guido Piovene wrote in the 1950's: "It is said that Milan is a utilitarian city, pulled down and rebuilt according to the needs of the moment, thus never managing to become old. It is true that every historical phase has left some trace of ugliness: the reign of Vittorio Emanuele II bequeathed us the Piazza del Duomo which has been defined as a 'monumental choreography arranged by bankers', later on the Fascist style of architecture was imposed on the city with utter disregard for nostalgia or memories, with its pompous facades, its marbles and vainglorious arches; still later the American style, more American than anything in America, with its sky-scrapers and mechanical toys. Despite all this, Milan is still a beautiful city. He who wanders along its streets with love can recognise, alongside buildings which may be offensive, many delightful and often ancient architectural treasures: there are the Romanesque basilicas of Sant'Ambrogio and Sant'Eustorgio; the touch of Bramante at Santa Maria delle Grazie and San Satiro; the Monastero Maggiore; Brera and the other museums, the Castello Sforzesco, the Ambrosiana, and the Poldi-Pezzoli. And then of course there is the Neo-classical Milan so admired by Stendhal...".

Stendhal: the French writer who loved Milan so much that he wished to have the adjective "Milanese" inscribed next to his name on his tomb. The author of *Chartreuse* claimed Milan was the "capital of music", and he wrote enthusiastic declarations of love about "La Scala", the world's temple of music. In his journal he noted: "Milan, 24th September. It was seven o'clock in the evening when I arrived, I was limp with exhaustion, but I dragged myself straight off to the Scala... and there, at one stroke, lay all the justification of my journey. My senses were so utterly weary that they were beyond the furthest reaches of pleasure. Yet all the fantasy that the most exotic intricacy of an oriental imagination may evolve, all that is most Baroque and bizarre, all that is most sumptuous in architectural devising, all that can be made to live and breathe through the soft brilliance of draperies, all that can be coaxed into reality through the symbolism of characters who have not merely the costume, but the very faces and gestures of their make-belief and alien lands... all this and more have I seen tonight." (Stendhal, *Rome, Naples and Florence in 1817).*

Lago Maggiore: Isola Bella, which is the most famous of the Borromean Islands, lies just off Stresa. Also known by the name Verbano, the lake (65 kilometres long and 2-10 kilometres wide) washes the shores of Lombardy, Piedmont (where this photograph was taken), and Switzerland.
Surrounded by magnificent mountain scenery, the area is also famous for its splendid villas and magnificent gardens.

Lago di Como, as seen from Villa Carlotta. This lake, which is also known as Lario, is considered to be one of the most fascinating in Europe. Some of its bays and coves, where the rocky cliffs plunge straight down into the blue-green waters, make one think of Capri, or some other Mediterranean island.
Formed by the River Adda, it divides into two parts at Como and Lecco. Made famous by Alessandro Manzoni, who set his novel *I Promessi Sposi* there, the lake is 50 kilometres long and at its widest point it is 4 kilometres wide. The noble villas of the 17th and 18th centuries which were built along its jagged shores attracted many famous visitors. Among the lakes well known resorts are those of Bellagio, Cernobbio, Tremezzo and Menaggio.

Turin: the Mole Antonelliana. Like the Gothic Duomo for Milan, the powerful Mole has become the traditional symbol of Turin. First conceived of as a Jewish synagogue and designed by the engineer Alessandro Antonelli (from whom it takes its name), the Mole was erected between the years 1863 and 1897, and soars up to a height of 167.50

metres. Its "spire", which is 45 metres high and topped by a star, had to be rebuilt after a tornado struck it in 1953. This extremely impressive but totally exaggerated structure provides a stark contrast to the organised grid-plan of the city below it (it is said that the mentality of the Torinese is similarly organised and somewhat rigid). Turin is an extremely industrious city and houses the factories of Fiat, making it the capital of the automobille industry in Italy; it is also an important cultural centre, albeit a conservative one, but its austerity is at the same time offset by a frivolous fin-de siècle atmosphere.

Valle d'Aosta, the Lago Blu mirrors the peak of the mighty Cervino, and the castle of Châtelard. We are in a corner of Italy where the mountain peaks, receding into the hazy distance behind each other as though they were painted onto the backdrop of some enormous stage, and the swirling soft mists of the valleys create an atmosphere of magic and peace. Towering above all this is Cervino which, when struck by the rays of the sun, shimmers and sparkles like some huge diamond. At 4,478 metres, Cervino is the third highest of the peaks in the Italian Alps (the highest is Monte Bianco or Mont Blanc, and then Monte Rosa).
These mountains have kindled the spirit of adventure and fantasy in generations of climbers, tempting them with their distant and awesome peaks, and the first man to conquer Cervino, or the Matterhorn as it is called by the Swiss, was the Englishman Edward Whymper in 1865. But his expedition paid very dearly for this triumph, for at the start of the descent four of his seven climbers plunged to their death down a glacier. The mountain has claimed many more lives since then, but it continues to fascinate and attract mountaineers from all over the world.
The Val D'Aosta is also a region of castles. Some are still intact and forbidding, others have disintegrated into ruins or are mere empty shells, whose gaunt walls and windows stand guard over the old twisting roads. Perched strategically on rocky outcrops, these hundred or so castles almost all date from the Middle Ages and are clearly visible from the floor of the valley and from the railway. At night, when they are illuminated, they look like something from a fairy tale, especially the castles of Fénis and of Saint Pierre.

Portofino. This is without doubt the most elegant, exclusive and famous place in Liguria. The fortunate inhabitants of the villas which look out over the small bay enjoy a view of truly outstanding beauty. It was this view which attracted the admiring gaze of Guy de Maupassant who, on one bright September morning in 1889, was sailing by on his yacht named "Bel Ami" after his famous novel. A plaque on the dock commemorates his subsequent disembarkation. And so, in 1953, in the *Corriere d'Informazione,* Orio Vergani wrote: "...Maupassant saw Portofino in its 'natural state' in the wonderful solitude of September. The arrival of the 'Bel Ami' proved to be quite an occasion as its inhabitants were only used to seeing the arrival and departure of the local fishing boats. The captain of the port appeared in person to catch the rope which Maupassant threw from the yacht. Small naked boys clambered around the rocks in the harbour, in fact it was exactly that sort of scene – pagan and somewhat Hellenic – which fitted in with the conventional image of Italy propagated by the poets of the last century. If the disembarkation had taken place at Tahiti instead of Portofino Maupassant would have probably received the same sort of impression...". Today no yacht, however luxurious, attracts more than a momentary glance from the inhabitants of Portofino, where now the beautiful people of the world have to compete to obtain a mooring. The town, however, is full of charm, rugged yet at the same time lush, a combination which almost unique.

San Fruttuoso. Nestling deep in the folds of the rocky coastline near the promontory of Portofino is another tiny, but very exclusive, fishing village, San Fruttuoso.
It enjoys a splendid location with marvellous views, but can only be reached by taking the boat which plies between Portofino and Santa Margherita. There has been a monastery here since the 8th century, and the Benedictine abbey which can be seen today dates from the 13th century.

Bordighera (Imperia). This is another well-known sea-side resort on the Ligurian Riviera di Ponente. The mild climate and luxuriant Mediterranean vegetation attract tourists from Italy and from other lands. A notable feature of the area is the extensive use of greenhouses which cover terraces and entire hill-sides. The mountains which ries up behind Bordighera and the other coastal towns of this region are very grim and forbidding; a complete contrast to the sweet and gentle landscape near the coast.

The Tuscan countryside. Tuscany is one of the most genuine and intimate areas of Italy; it has inspired and moved some of the greatest artists in the world. The Tuscan countryside is not just something that can be glanced at, for it is a work of art itself, created by the passing of the centuries. To visit the Val del Chianti, to take just one example, is like wandering around an art gallery filled with pictures celebrating one theme – landscapes: the countryside in chiaroscuro, furrowed by the plough, or occupied by orderly armies of vines which yield a wine which is the envy of the whole world. Among these picturesque hills one often comes across farmhouses which have been restored by lovers of the area, and also many ancient villas and castles, precious reminders of an exciting and colourful past.

Florence, the Lungo Arno viewed from Piazzale Michelangelo. Obviously the blood-red sunset has added to the breathtaking beauty of this view of the city, but the charm of

Florence and its legendary river is not only due to its admittedly impressive scenographic qualities. Florence, together with Venice and Rome, is one of Italy's foremost cities of art. This photograph has managed to capture several of her more important monuments: Ponte Vecchio, Palazzo degli Uffizi, and Santa Maria del Fiore. This city has such an intense concentration of works of art that several psychologists have suggested that it might be the cause of a type of nervous breakdown. None of this has actually been proved or scientifically demonstrated, but it would seem that people who are of a sensitive nature become confused and disoriented when confronted with such an amazing concentration of beautiful achitecture, paintings and sculpture. This confused state is known as the "Stendhal Syndrome", in memory of the famous French writer who experienced just such a breakdown on 22nd January 1817, while visiting the tombs in Santa Croce.

Florence, the church of Santa Maria del Fiore (the Duomo, or Cathedral). On the left can be seen Giotto's bell-tower, and in the centre the dome designed by Brunelleschi. To the right one can just see the Palazzo della Signoria, the municipal town hall. This most elegant combination of ecclesiastical and civil architecture confers an extremely noble and totally Italian aspect to the city. Henry James, in his *Italian Hours* noted "The more I look at the old Florentine domestic architecture the more I like it – that of the great examples at least; and if I am ever able to build myself a lordly pleasure house I don't see how in conscience I can build it different from these."

Florence, Ponte Vecchio on the Arno. The only one of Florence's medieval bridges to be spared by the Nazis during their retreat in 1944, the Ponte Vecchio has become, like Venice's Bridge of Sighs, a meeting-place for those in love. The whole structure is lined with tiny boutiques selling jewellery, some of which is good, and some not so good!

Florence, Palazzo degli Uffizi with a copy of Michelangelo's *David* in the foreground (the original can be seen in the Galleria della Accademia). Built according to plans drawn up by Vasari for Cosimo I in 1500, the Palazzo degli Uffizi houses one of the most important museums in the world. Unless one has the time to spend several days just wandering around the Palazzo's galleries, it is simply not possible to see every painting and piece of sculpture exhibited here. Amongst the museum's masterpieces are works by Cimabue, Masaccio, Botticelli, Signorelli, Perugino, Dürer, Cranach, Giovanni Bellini, Giorgione, Correggio, Michelangelo, Parmigianino, Paolo Veronese, Tintoretto, Caravaggio, Rubens, and Rembrandt.

Florence, San Miniato al Monte. A jewel of Florentine Romanesque, San Miniato was built in the 11th and 12th centuries. Its outstanding position and extremely elegant green and white marble facade make it one of the city's most admired monuments. Here can be seen works by Taddeo Gaddi, Luca della Robbia, Paolo Uccello, and Andrea del Castagno.

Florence, Galleria degli Uffizi: *The birth of Venus* by Sandro Botticelli.

Florence, the Boboli Gardens: the decorated Grotto. "The Boboli Gardens are not large – you wonder how compact little Florence finds room for them within her walls," said Henry James. He added, "But they are scattered to their extreme, their all romantic advantage and felicity, over steep undulations between the rugged and terraced palace and a still-surviving stretch of city wall, where the unevenness of the ground much adds to their apparent size."

Designed by Triboli, an expert landscape gardener, every year the Boboli Gardens are host to the *Maggio Musicale Fiorentino*.

Pisa, the Duomo and the Campanile, the Baptistry and the Camposanto are collectively known as the Campo dei Miracoli (Field of Miracles), and indeed the green lawns do seem to unfold and reveal before our eyes these miracles of architecture. Here, next to each other, are the four masterpieces which to Henry James appeared as "ancient ivories, wonderfully wrought". The Cathedral, consecrated in 1118, is an exquisite example of architectural composition: the Baptistry, in part the outcome of the genius of Giovanni and Nicola Pisano; then there is the most famous tower in world, which seems just about to topple over (but do not be too distracted by the alarming angle of the building – admire for a while the harmony of the balustrades and the delightful play of chiaroscuro); lastly the Camposanto, white and serene, considered by many to be the most beautiful and moving cemetery on the world, thanks to the many works of art within its walls. Some of these were destroyed during the terrible bombing raids of 1944, when for 40 days the city shook as the Germans on one side of the river and the Allies on the other tried to annihilate each other.

San Gimignano (Siena). This small town has managed to preserve its mediaeval architecture which dates mostly from the 12th and 13th centuries, an age when there arose a veritable forest of towers to proclaim their builders' wealth and social standing. At one time the city bristled with more than seventy of these towers, whereas now they number a mere thirteen, but San Gimignano still possesses a unique character which attracts crowds of tourists to enjoy the charm of its ancient stones and its delicious wines. The crenellated battlements which crown the city walls were originally constructed to repel visitors, now they serve only to attract them.

Siena, Piazza del Campo. In his *Viaggio in Italia* Guido Piovene tells us how that great art historian Bernard Berensen described Siena: "A unique work of art which knows no parallel in our western world, a complete animal, with a head, heart, arteries, and legs, whose skeleton is almost intact, resting on three hills." Of this "unique work of art" – certainly somewhat different from the days when Berensen first contemplated it due to a not always judicious insertion of offices and appartments in the venerable fabric of this city of art – Piazza del Campo provides the ideal synthesis. It is as though the architects had set up an enormous shell in the heart of the city and had constructed all around it magnificent palaces, with the Palazzo Pubblico at its centre, all of this overlooked by the Torre del Mangia (so-called after the nick-name of a certain Giovanni di Duccio who used to strike the hours). A theatre-piazza like many others in Italy, this one is famous because of the Palio horse-race which is held there, one of the most exciting and colourful horse-races in the world: the horses and heroes from all the different *contrade* or *quartieri* of the city gallop at incredible speed three times around the square in an attempt to snatch the ancient prize from their enemies. The Palio is run twice a year, on 2nd July and 16th August.

Assisi, Basilica of San Francesco (the Upper Church). The warmest heart of Italy beats in the streets of this city, where the marks and scars of history are surrounded by a rich and abundant country-side. Here, among the black cypresses and silver-leaved olive groves, the mediaeval preachers founded centres of culture which today attract tourists in their thousands. This city, whose ancient walls are garlanded with flowers, constantly reminds one of the saint who gave his name to the magnificent basilica, Francesco. His memory lives on in the peaceful atmosphere of the town, the sweet mildness of the rolling hills, and in the picturesque meanderings of the narrow streets.

It was while wandering in those very streets, however, that Wolfgang Goethe received a surprise that was anything but sweet, and which he did not omit to mention in his *Viaggio in Italia*. Walking alone one evening in the dark whilst his groom went on ahead with the carriage, the great German writer was approached by figures, two of whom were armed. These men blocked his way and demanded to know who he was and what he was doing walking alone at night. "I replied," recounts Goethe, "that I was a foreigner to those parts and that I was walking the streets of Assis whilst my groom proceeded me with my cariage towards Foligno." He adds, "It seemed to them impossible that a traveller would pay for a carriage and then proceed on foot. They asked me if I had already visited the Gran Convento. I said that I had not, reassuring them however that I had known about it for some time, but being an architect, I was at the moment only interested in Santa Maria della Minerva which, as they well knew, was a masterpiece. Of course they could not contradict me but they were very perturbed that I had not paid my tribute of devotion to the patron Saint...". This episode not only illustrates the prevalent architectural tastes of the great German intellectual at that time, but also demonstrates the reverence in which the citizens hold their saint and the church which contains his remains. In this basilica one can admire wonderful frescoes by Giotto, Cimabue, Lorenzetti, and Simone Martini.

Urvieto, a view of the interior of the Duomo. Built to commemorate the miracle of Balsena (in 1263, whilst a priest was celebrating mass, blood dripped from a consecrated host), this must be one of the most beautiful churches in Christendom. From its extraordinary facade which was rearranged in the 14th century and enriched by Andrea Orcagna's splendid rose-windows, to the most intimate yet perfect detail of its interior, it is the delightful result of the combination of Romanesque and Gothic architecture. Particularly noteworthy are the reliquaries of S.S. Corporale, the frescoes by Gentile da Fabriano, Pinturicchio, Beato Angelico, and Luca Signorelli. The Pozzo di San Patrizio (St. Patrick's Well) attracts crowds of visitors.
This Umbrian town in the province of Terni sits spectacularly on top of a tufa.

Rome, St. Peter's Square and the Via della Conciliazione. The heir to the patrimony of the Roman Empire, the Church has made Rome the world centre of Christianity. People from every nation gather together in this vast square, which Bernini surrounded with an elipse of columns, like two arms reaching out in a welcoming embrace, when the Pope appears on his balcony to talk and to bless his flock. The obelisk at the centre of this enormous area comes from ancient Egypt. In the 17th century two fountains were erected, the one on the right, looking towards the basilica, is by Carlo Maderno, who also designed the facade of St. Peter's.
The Basilica, built over the tomb of the Holy Apostle, was first built by the Emperor Constantine in 326. The re-construction, begun in 1506, attracted some of the most famous geniuses in the world of art: Bramante, Raphael, Antonio da Sangallo, Michelangelo, and Maderno. The interior is like a cavernous jewellery-box which contains masterpieces too important to be discussed briefly here.

Rome, Piazza Navona and the Trinità dei Monti. Here are two of Rome's most favourite places which are always full of tourists; to make a rendez-vous in the Baroque Piazza Navona or on the flower-covered Spanish Steps, or in front of the Trevi Fountain means putting yourself in a particular state of mind, that same state which suggested to Stendhal – who, it must be admitted, was not a great admirer of Rome, and especially of its Catholic architecture – the famous phrase: "The ideal would be an active life, alternated with periods of repose with the pleasure of the sweet climate of Rome."

Urbino, the Palazzo Ducale. This 15th century building is perhaps one of the most beautiful buildings in Italy. Largely the work of the architect Luciano Laurana, the Palace is a manifestation of the glory of the Montefeltro family who dominated Urbino, and whose principal figure was Federico (1444-1482). The famous literary critic Mario Praz writes in his *Il mondo che ho visto* "...to arrive at Urbino after having crossed over a countryside which, from Fossato di Vico to the Furlo Pass, seems like one of those barren landscapes painted by Giotto, and find oneself in front of the magnificent and elegant triple loggia flanked by strong slim towers looking just like minarets...".
The Palazzo Ducale houses the Galleria nazionale delle Marche; amongst its many treaures are the female portrait by Raphael, who was born in Urbino, which goes by the name of *La Muta;* Melozzo da Forli's *Cristo;* Paolo Uccello's *Profanazione dell'Ostia;* the *Flagellazione and Madonna* by Piero della Francesca; *L'ultima cena* and the *Resurrezione* by Titian. Some splendid tarsia which have been attributed to Botticelli can be seen the room known as "The Study of Duke Ferdinand".

Rome, the Tiber with Castel Sant'Angelo on the right and Michelangelo's dome of St. Peter's in the background. When you get tired of wandering around Rome's countless museums, go for a stroll along the banks of the Tiber whose waters may no longer be as limpid as they used to be but which still, however, retain their ancient charm. Walking alongside the river you can reflect upon the amazing mélange of styles which make up the Rome of today – Classical, Mediaeval, Renaissance, Baroque, Rococo, Neoclassical, and then everything which may be called modern or Post-Modern; in short, Rome is a metropolis of a thousand faces, of a thousand moods. Here, behind these scarred but still noble walls, civilizations have been piled up one on top of another, creating a compact and well-knit mass: this is a city which reads like a history book.

Rome, Arch of Titus, with the Forum, and the interior of the Colosseum. Today they are simply ruins, however romantic they may seem to be, but what a glorious and powerful past they have had! From this Forum the Romans ruled their vast empire. Under magnificent arches like that of Titus or between the imposing or slender columns of temples whose fallen stones litter this space which is consecrated to the misty past, marched glorious legions returning from far away lands. And after every victory there were parades and games which took place in that immense amphitheatre called the Colosseum. This was built for Vespasianus but finished in 800 B.C. by his son Titus, the Emperor who destroyed Jerusalem. Fifty-seven metres high with three orders of arches, the Colosseum could hold 50,000 spectators.

Paestum, the Basilica (6th century B.C.). A Greek city dedicated to the god Neptune, Paestum (originally Poseidonia) was built on the plain of Sele, about 40 kilometres south of Salerno. For many hundreds of years buried under swamps and brushwood, the monumental complex only came to light again in 1700. Among the magnificent architectural remains which can be seen today are those of the Basilica, the Temple of Neptune (one of the most beautiful of all Doric temples), and the Temple of Ceres.

Pompeii, a fresco in the Villa dei Misteri. This large fresco illustrates a scene from the initiation rites to the Dionysian mysteries. The Villa dei Misteri, like other important monuments and private homes on the site, was discovered during the excavations which have been carried out uninterruptedly since 1748. Pompeii, like Herculaneum, was completely destroyed by the eruption of Vesuvius, on whose slopes they were built, in 79 A.D. A torrential rain of ashes and molten lava buried every house, man and beast. The eruption was so sudden and definitive that archeologists have unearthed petrified cadavers of human beings whose wretched expressions and gestures, "frozen" for eternity, show in vivid, horrible detail their death throes, and their dreadful suffering.
The Lupanare, a sort of brothel, attracts many curious tourists who come to gaze at its decidedly licentious decorations.

Pompeii, archeological excavations. The city was founded in the 8th century B.C. by the Osci, an ancient Italic people, but came later under Greek and Etruscan dominion. Conquered by the Romans in 89 B.C., Pompeii lived a period of splendour as a busy port and rich commercial centre.

Ischia, the beach of Sant'Angelo. Of volcanic origin, Ischia is the largest of the islands which embellish the Gulf of Naples. Its thermal springs have always been one of the islands principal attractions. Of the countless descriptions praising the beauty of the island we have chosen that of the Touring Club Italiano as being most apt... "The realisation that one is on volcanic land hits one as soon as one moves away from the various bars, restaurants, hotels and boutiques which surround the harbour. It's enough to enter the splendid gardens, which were opened to the public only a few years ago, and see the twisted lumps of black lava, around which grow lush and splendid vegetation and flowers, marvellous examples of maritime pines, gigantesque plane trees, oaks and chestnuts. As in all areas which have volcanic origins the flora tends to be larger than normal, but the same cannot be said for the fauna, which is almost non-existent apart from the sea-gulls swooping around the harbour and a few jackdaws which wheel slowly around the castle. In order to see wild-birds it is necessary to climb up towards Mount Epomeo, whose lower slopes are covered with vines which gradually give way to chestnut trees the higher one climbs. From several vantage points it is possible to have an extraordinary view of Ischia, with its narrow streets, crystal waters and blindingly white houses. Down below there is a greyish patch which marks the place where excavations are being carried out on the site of Phitecussa, the oldest Greek colony in the Gulf of Naples, dating from the 7th century B.C. Not far away one can see the large cistern built by the Romans and transformed into the first Christian church on the island. From Mount Epomeo one can see the island of Capri...".

Capri, the precipitous Faraglioni. This is one of the most famous islands in the world; it has inspired poets and artists from every age. "Beautiful, horrible, haunted, that is the essence of what, about itself, Capri says to you," writes Henry James in his *Italian Hours*. Beautiful, horrible, haunted: Capri is an island whose physical beauty and geographical location has attracted both friend and foe, aesthetes and barbarians.
The Emperor Tiberius lived here and indeed governed the Roman Empire from here from 27 to 37 A.D. The ruins of his palace look out onto one of the most spectacular and extraordinary panoramas that nature can possibly offer. At Capri the vegetation is lush, and "inland" (Anacapri) the landscape becomes decidedly rural; this is where the island reveals its "peasant" character.
From a promontory which is almost inaccesible to those who are travelling on foot, called Capo Masullo, the writer Curzio Malaparte built his famous villa – a monument to his mania for grandeur, to his need to shock and astonish. Malaparte would have liked his villa to be used by Chinese students but today it is the property of a foundation called "Giorgio Ronchi", after Malaparte's nephew who was killed by a hand-grenade in the Second World War.
The meeting-place for the international set is of course Piazza Umberto I, more well known as the Piazzetta. In the summer the Blue Grotto, with its shimmering incandescent light-effects, enchants whole armies of tourists. Capri, like all other well-known tourist spots, is best visited out of season if possible; in the spring one can admire all the splendour of nature in peace, and in autumn, when the summer rush has died down, it is heavenly to wile away the hours just gazing at the scenery or out to sea, or perhaps trying to get a glimpse of that mythical lizard which lives only on the rocks of Capri.

dary brigands and heroes, where the folklore is not a dry subject only fit for anthropological research but a theme of everyday life.

Costiera Sorrentina (Ravello) and Costiera Amalfitana (Positano). Two stretches of the Italian coastline where Nature seems to have surpassed herself in beauty. Unfortunately the expansion of modern means of transport has disturbed the tranquility of these delectable paradises where the sirens used to sing, but even today a visit there will remain in one's memory for ever.

The names of two famous musicians are connected with Ravello: Wagner began to compose *Parsifal* whilst on a visit, and Grieg conceived his *Lieder* here. After having visited the Arabic-Norman monuments and having passed through the terraced vineyard one arrives at Villa Cimbrone, whose belvedere can boast the most wonderful view of the Gulf of Salerno. Villa Rufolo is another famous tourist attraction.

Until quite recently Positano was just another small, but admittedly beautiful, fishing village; now it has become one of the most exclusive resorts on the Italian coast, beloved by such writers as Paul Klee and Tennessee Williams. I have stolen from Darwin Porter, author of the famous *Dollarwise Guide to Italy* a quotation which refers to John Steinbeck and which seems particularly appropriate to me: "Positano reaches the innermost parts. It is a place of dreams which is not really real even when one is actually there, and whose 'call' becomes real only after one has left." This is the sort of feeling one often gets in Italy, especially here in the South: its beauty is perfectly objective, totally visible, yet still mysterious.

Puglia, faraglione (isolated crags of rock) in the Bay of the Zagare, on the Gargano. Strangely shaped rocks plunge down into a lapis lazuli sea or tumble down onto the beach in chaotic primordial confusion. This is a part of Puglia clearly blessed by Nature. Even though the interior is is well worth visiting, it is the magnificent coastline of the Gargano which attracts visitors in their hundreds of thousands every year. Across the deep blue Adriatic lies the Dalmatian coast and the mysterious land of Albania.

Puglia, Ostuni. This sun-bleached town in the province of Brindisi is just one of the many attractions of a region whose natural beauty provides a perfect backdrop to some incomparable architectural monuments (the Cathedral of Trani, Castel de Monte, the Cathedral of Ruvo, the marvellous Baroque architecture of Lecce). This is the area of the *trulli* (especially famous are those of Alberobello), strange beehive-like buildings built of stone.

Puglia is considered to be the least "southern" of the regions in the south of Italy, but just how many "souths" are there, and how many "norths?" Italy changes all the time, each kilometre is different from the one which preceded it, and from the one which will follow it: landscape, colours, forms, even moods, all differ. Even the inhabitants of the various provinces and towns differ from each other, moving across the stage recounting their own history in their own language. This is the extraordinary thing about Italy, every individual community is a flourishing cultural centre with its own peculiarities and characteristics. It has been like this ever since the time of the *comuni,* who proclaimed their independence and defended it ferociously from the fortified walls of their cities.

Basilicata, Rivello. This town look as though it is literally, and dramatically, clinging to the edge of a cliff, surrounded by mountains which have at the same time protected and isolated it. Rivello, like the other towns in the Basilicata (which was known as Lucania until 1947), seems to give the impression that it has only just been discovered by the traveller, for during the 18th and 19th centuries, when all the visitors to Italy were making their almost obligatory stops at the more fashionable and accessible towns, it was more or less ignored. It is true that isolation can result in under-development, but on the other hand it does help preserve old customs and ancient rites and the survival of that quintessential peasant culture which has all but disappeared from the rest of Italy.

To wander around these valleys is to experience the most ancient Italy, a land of legen-

Isola di Lipari (Sicily). The stark white of the floating pumice-stone contrasts sharply with the azure blue of the Tyrrhenian Sea. Lipari, together with Stromboli, Salina, Vulcano, Filicudi, Alicudi, and Panarea make up the Eolian Archipelago, north of Capo Milazzo. The volcanic nature of these small islands gives them a rather wild look. Black lava rocks look even blacker against the bright white pumice-stone, and the sulphorous fumes rising up out of the rocks all add to the islands' mysterious aura. Small, hidden coves with beautifully clear and clean water will delight those bathers who have been driven away from other popular Italian beaches by the threat of pollution.

Cefalù. This is one of the most remarkable stretches of the Sicilian coast, and when one speaks of this region one is usually referring to the sea. This is not so common as one might think because although Sicily is an island its inhabitants are much more at home on land than they are at sea; they have had to defend themselves and their land from repeated raids and attacks from the sea so perhaps this is why their hearts lean more inland, to the dry plains and barren mountains. It is interesting to note that very little of the enormous quantity of Sicilian literature actually ever mentions the sea, and in one of the rare cases in which it does feature, in Verga's *I Malavoglia,* it is seen more of a punishment on the part of Nature rather than a gift.

Therefore Cefalù is one of the few sea-side resorts in Sicily. Its Norman-Arabian cathedral is one of the great monuments in the western world.

Taormina, the Greek Theatre with Mount Etna in the background. The characteristic elements of Sicily – the sea, mountains, and ancient monuments – are all to be found at Taormina which, from its high vantage point, looks out over the Ionian Sea from whence arrived the first Greek ship in 735 B.C. When speaking about the island two centuries ago Wolfgang Goethe wrote: "...without Sicily it is not possible to have any real idea of Italy. Here lies the key to everything...". In its turn Taormina can be seen as the key to Sicily, as its prestigious symbol. But once again let Goethe guide us through the marvellous arhitectural macchinations of the Greek Theatre: "After having passed by the rocks, which rise up not far from the beach, there are two peaks which are connected by a semicircle. Whatever was the natural structure, it is a fact that art has helped and has shaped that semi-circle in the form of an amphitheatre, for the comfort of the spectators; walls and other constructions in brick have furnished corridors and all the necessary rooms; at the foot of the steps of the semi-circle a stage has been constructed, which, having joined together the two rocky walls, has completed the greatest work of nature and of art. He who stands at the highest point, occupied at one time by the spectators, cannot but confess that perhaps never has any audience had such a spectacle before their eyes....".

Agrigento, Temple of Concordia. This is one of the most significant monuments from the Greek civilization in Sicily. The temple, with its Doric columns, was called *Concordia* after an inscription in Latin which was uncovered during excavations. This building, which time has treated very gently and which has used as a Christian church up to the 17th century, stands on a steep hill half-way between the modern town of Agrigento and the sea. The hills around this area boast the remains of other magnificent temples dedicated to various Greek deities such as Juno Lacinia, Hercules, and Zeus (obviously a very important building, recent attempts to reconstruct it on a reduced scale have shown the vastness of the complex). The Temple of the Dioscures (the Heavenly Twins) concludes, in the west, the archeological tour of the Valley of Temples, an immense patrimony of history, insanely and criminally besieged by appartment buildings and holiday homes which, at Agrigento, huddle up against each other in squalid disorder. But it's enough to get away by oneself to the Valley to realise that one is in a magical, mystical environment, where the history is written in the very stones which the centuries-old olive trees and patient almonds all but hide away from view; and in the tranquility of long dead civilizations the words of Quasimodo will enrich and expand our thoughts: *"Là dura un vento che ricordo acceso / nelle criniere dei cavalli obliqui / in corsa lungo le pianure, vento / che macchia e / rode l'arenaria e il cuore / dei telamoni lugubri, riversi / sopra l'erba...".* (The manes of the horses racing over the plains, straining and leaning forward, are whipped by a wind which will never cease.

A wind which stains and erodes the sandstone and the hearts of the mournful Telemones, now cast down to the ground).

Sardinia, two views of the Costa Smeralda (in the large photograph – Porto Cervo). Due to the efforts and financial backing of the Aga Khan, this stretch of Sardinian coast, which not too many years ago was a rocky bay frequented by goats and the occasional goat-herd, is now an area dedicated to the needs and desires of the rich, the famous, and the beautiful. "A land which has never been conquered," wrote D.H. Lawrence of this island. Because of its proud character and invincible insularity it is like no other region in Italy.

"Whether one disembarks at Olbia or Cagliari, or at Porto Torres, Sardinia always gives the impression of another continent, with shapes, colours, light and landscape quite different from those we are used to...", one reads in a chapter of the Touring Club Guide dedicated to this island of *nuraghe*. "Perhaps it is really a remnant of the mythical Tyrrhenide which has survived an immense cataclysm similar to the one which vanquished the lost and equally mythical continent of Atlantis, or else an enormous rocky raft of land which broke away from the earth's crust on a sea of molten magma billions of years ago. The Bay of Olbia, enclosed in the distance by the granite Gallura mountains and to the southwest by the enormous limestone prism of the island of Tavolara, in particular reminds one very much of the far off lands of Australia."

But like Sicily, it is not just the coastline of Sardinia which merits our attention. The interior is rich in customs and rituals which have remained unchanged for centuries, as has the Sardinian language, a tongue which is all but comprehensible to the multitudes of Italian tourists who invade the island every year.

Photo Credits

All the photographs which appear in this book are
by H. Simeone Huber, with the exceptions
of the following:
Venice, Ca' d'Oro - Paolo Marton
Turin, Mole Antonelliana - Mario De Biasi
San Gimignano - Fabio Santagiuliana
Assisi, Basilica of San Francesco - Elio Ciol
Rome, Piazza Navona - Paolo Marton